Hala

For Muslims around the World

BY

Rachael Rayner

License Notes

No part of this Book can be reproduced in any form or by any means including print, electronic, scanning or photocopying unless prior permission is granted by the author.

All ideas, suggestions and guidelines mentioned here are written for informative purposes. While the author has taken every possible step to ensure accuracy, all readers are advised to follow information at their own risk. The author cannot be held responsible for personal and/or commercial damages in case of misinterpreting and misunderstanding any part of this Book

Table of Contents

Introduction

Muslims around the world eat significant amount of meat all through the year. It is quite uncommon to find vegetarian Muslims. They have a special ritual to make their meat Halal. They need to pray to Allah (GOD) before slaughtering the animals. If they do not supplicate before slaughtering, the meat does not become halal. If you are a Muslim, and living in a non-Muslim country, whenever you are buying meat, you need to make sure it is Halal meat. Muslims do not eat Pork, Wine, Beer, or any types of alcohols. So, any type of alcohol and pork should not be in their cooking either.

Muslims do not eat blood either. So, make sure to wash off the blood completely from the meat and then cook it.

Check the labels of each product. Chocolates, pastries, beverages, chewing gums, candies and gelatin have pork fat in them. So, whenever you are grocery shopping, make sure to buy pork fat free items and alcohol free items. There are halal beef fat substitutes available in most shops. Muslims love dates, figs, goat milk and pomegranate. You will see a lot of these ingredients in their daily meals.

It is safe to eat all kinds of fish for Muslims. So, when you are going seafood shopping, you do not have to worry about checking anything. This book contains a mixture of breakfast, main courses, snacks and desserts for a week. They are both simple and complex recipes to give you an idea about the Halal foodies out there. If you are a new cook, you can start from the simple recipes and then as you grow, you can try the advance recipes later.

Breakfast

Wild Blueberry and Pomegranate Smoothie

Muslims love pomegranate. It has a lot of health benefits. Start your day with this smoothie and your day will be very productive.

Serving Size: 2

Ingredients:

- 1 cup wild blueberries
- 1 cup pomegranate seeds
- 1 cup goat milk
- A pinch of salt
- Fresh mint
- 4-5 ice cubes

Instructions:

1. In a blender add the fruits.

2. Add the mint, salt, goat milk and ice cubes.

3. Blend until you get a smooth mix.

4. Serve cold.

Yogurts with Fruits

Yogurt is very good for the health. Adding fruits to it makes the breakfast more healthy and wholesome. Add any fruits of your choice to this yogurt.

Serving Size: 2 cups

Ingredients:

- 2 cup low carb yogurt
- 1 kiwi cut into slices
- 1 tbsp blueberry compote
- 2 tbsp basil seeds
- 1 cup water

Instructions:

1. In a bowl add the basil seeds. Pour water on top and let it sit for 10 minutes.

2. In serving cups, arrange the kiwi slices.

3. Pour in half of the yogurt.

4. Add the soaked basil seeds. Add the remaining yogurt.

5. Add the blueberry compote. Serve cold.

Breakfast Cranberry Orange Bread

Are you tired of eating the same bread all the time? It is time to add a new spin to your regular breads. Add orange, cranberries in it and see how magical it becomes! I often make this bread and my family loves it in their breakfast.

Serving Size: 16 slices

Cooking Time: 20 Minutes

Ingredients:

- 1/2 cup all purpose flour
- 4 egg yolks
- 1/3 cup cranberries
- ¼ cup butter
- 1 pinch of orange zest
- 2 tbsp sugar
- 1 tsp baking powder
- 1 drop of orange extract
- 1 cup cream cheese
- A pinch of salt

Instructions:

1. In a mixing bowl whisk the egg yolks.

2. Mix in cream cheese. Whisk for 2 minutes.

3. Add the butter, sugar and whisk for another 2 minutes.

4. Now add the orange extract and the orange zest. Mix well.

5. Finally shift in the dry Ingredients:.

6. Fold gently using a spatula. Add the cranberries and fold.

7. Pour the mix into your prepared loaf pan.

8. Bake for 30 minutes with 350 degrees F.

9. When it cools down, cut into slices and serve with tea or coffee.

10. You can add cream cheese drizzle on top If you like.

Raspberry Pancake

Pancake is the ultimate breakfast choice around the world. It is very versatile as anyone can make it their own by adding their own choice of fruits and flour. I have used raspberries here.

Serving Size: 2

Cooking Time: 10 Minutes

Ingredients:

- 2 tbsp raspberry compote
- 2 eggs
- 1 cup flour
- 2 tbsp olive oil
- A pinch of salt
- 2 tbsp butter
- ¼ cup goat milk
- 2 tbsp honey
- Fresh raspberries to serve

Instructions:

1. In a big mixing bowl, beat the eggs until they are light and fluffy.

2. Add the sugar and mix well.

3. Add the raspberry compote and oil and mix again.

4. Finally add the flour, salt and fold gently.

5. In a pan melt the butter and fry the pancakes golden brown in batches.

6. Serve with fresh fruits on top.

Coconut Porridge

Porridge is one of the comfort food around the world. It is easy to make. It is very nutritious. You can add any fruits of your choice here. I have added figs, blueberries and raspberries.

Serving Size: 2

Cooking Time: 10 Minutes

Ingredients:

- 1 cup shredded coconut
- 2 cup goat milk
- 1 tsp coconut butter
- 4 tbsp oats
- A pinch of salt
- ¼ tsp coconut extract
- Figs and raspberries to serve

Instructions:

1. Combine the goat milk with shredded coconut in a pot.

2. Add the coconut extract, oil and mix well.

3. Fold in the dry Ingredients: and mix until there are no lumps. Cook on low heat for 10 minutes.

4. Take off the heat and wait for it to cool down.

5. Serve with fresh figs, blueberries and raspberries on top.

Avocado Coconut Nutty Goat milkshake

Smoothies are filled with nutrition. They are perfect to boost your energy level. If you have one glass of this milkshake, you will be fine for the next 2 hours.

Serving Size: 1

Ingredients:

- 1 ripe avocado
- 1 cup goat milk
- 3-4 dates
- 1 tsp crushed almonds
- A pinch of salt
- Fresh mint

Instructions:

1. Cut the dates in half and discard the pit. Add to a blender.

2. Peel the avocado and discard the pit.

3. Chop it and add to the blender.

4. Pour in the goat milk, salt, mint and crushed almonds.

5. Blend for 1 minute. Serve cold.

Savory Veggie French toast

French toast is something you can prepare within 5 minutes and it tastes quite good. People usually make sweet French toast, but I have made savory French toast here.

Serving Size: 2

Cooking Time: 10 Minutes

Ingredients:

- 2 eggs
- 4 slices of white bread
- Salt and black pepper to taste
- 2 tbsp olive oil or butter
- 1 tbsp flour
- ¼ cup chopped broccoli florets
- ½ onion, chopped
- 1 green chili, chopped
- ¼ cup spinach, chopped
- Fresh coriander, chopped

Instructions:

1. In a mixing bowl whisk the eggs.

2. Add the flour, veggies, salt, pepper, and chili. Mix well.

3. In a pan heat the oil or butter.

4. Dip the bread slices into the mixture and fry them golden brown from both sides.

5. Repeat the process with all the bread slices.

Main Course

Stuffed Avocado with Tuna

Avocado is very nutritious as tuna! When you combine the two, this becomes a powerful dish. It can be served as a breakfast and a good brunch as well.

Serving Size: 2

Cooking Time: 30 Minutes

Ingredients:

- 1 avocado
- 1 cup tuna meat
- Salt and pepper to taste
- 1 tsp oil
- 1 tomato, diced
- 1 red onion, diced
- 1 green chili, diced
- ½ tsp chopped rosemary

Instructions:

1. Cut the avocado in half. Discard the seed. Set aside for now.

2. In a pan heat the oil. Add the onion and fry for 1 minute.

3. Add the tomato and fry for 2 minutes.

4. Add the tuna meat, sprinkle the salt, pepper and toss for 5 minutes.

5. Add the chili, rosemary and toss for another 2 minutes.

6. Stuff the avocado pieces with the tuna mix.

7. Bake in the oven for 20 minutes with 350 degrees F.

Soya Chunks with Bell Pepper

Soya chunks are very good protein option for people who enjoys vegetarian food. I often make this dish and my family loves it. I have added bell pepper here. Adding cauliflower or carrots would work well in the recipe too.

Serving Size: 2

Cooking Time: 30 minutes

Ingredients:

- 1 cup soya chunks
- ½ cup diced green bell pepper
- 1 onion, diced
- 1 green chili
- Salt and pepper to taste
- 1 tsp butter
- 1 tsp soy sauce
- 1 tsp tomato puree

Instructions:

1. Boil the soya chunks for 10 minutes.

2. Drain well and wash with cold water. Squeeze out the water from it.

3. In a pan melt the butter.

4. Add the onion and fry for a minute.

5. Add the soya chunks, soy sauce, tomato puree and ½ cup of water.

6. Cover with lid and cook for 5 minutes.

7. Add the chilies, salt, pepper and bell pepper.

8. Cook for another 5 minutes. Serve hot.

Mushroom Risotto

Who does not like risotto? Mushroom risotto is easy to make and tastes very good. You can be creative and add more vegetables like cabbage, onion, and carrot too.

Serving Size: 2

Cooking Time: 30 Minutes

Ingredients:

- 1 cup dried brown mushroom
- 1 cup brown rice
- 2 tbsp butter
- White pepper to taste
- ¼ cup goat milk
- 1 onion, diced
- 1 cup mushroom stock
- Salt to taste

Instructions:

1. Soak the dried mushrooms in warm water for 20 minutes.

2. Drain and set aside for now.

3. In a skillet melt the butter.

4. Fry the onion, mushroom for 1 minute.

5. Add the rest of the ingredients. Stir well and bring it to boil.

6. Simmer for 10 minutes.

7. Serve hot.

Vegetarian Casserole

Everyone enjoys casserole because it takes little preparation and it tastes delicious. Even if you make it vegetarian, if you follow this recipe, you family will not miss the meat with this dish.

Serving Size: 4

Cooking Time: 1 hour

Ingredients:

- 1 cup broccoli florets, diced
- 2 eggs
- 1 cup goat milk
- Fresh basil
- ½ cup diced raw papaya
- 2 tbsp olive oil
- 1 cup parmesan cheese
- ½ cup mozzarella cheese
- 2 red onion, diced
- 1 tsp oregano
- 1 cup potatoes, diced
- Salt and pepper to taste

Instructions:

1. Preheat your oven to 400 degrees F.

2. Use cooking spray on your casserole dish.

3. In a skillet, add olive oil over medium heat.

4. Add the onion and cook for 1 minute.

5. Add the potato, broccoli and papaya. Stir for 5 minutes.

6. Add the veggies into the casserole dish.

7. In another bowl whisk the eggs.

8. Add the parmesan cheese, mozzarella cheese, goat milk, oregano, salt and pepper.

9. Pour onto the veggies. Add the basil leaves on top.

10. Bake for 1 hour in the oven.

Spicy Noodles and Meatball

Noodles and meatballs cannot go wrong. I have used ground chicken for the meatballs. You can use ground beef, ground turkey, or any other meat of your choice.

Serving Size: 2

Cooking Time: 30 Minutes

Ingredients:

- 10 oz ramen noodles
- 1 cup ground chicken
- ½ cup black beans, boiled
- 2 white onion, chopped
- 1 red onion, diced
- 1/3 cup chicken stock
- ½ cup olive oil
- 1 egg
- Salt and pepper to taste
- ½ tsp chopped oregano
- ½ tsp chopped coriander
- 1 chili, chopped
- 1 cup tomato sauce

Instructions:

1. In a pan add some oil and fry the ground chicken until brown.

2. Mash the boiled black beans finely. Combine with the ground chicken mix.

3. Add the white onion, eggs, coriander, salt, pepper and mix well.

4. Use your hands to create meatballs.

5. In a skillet add some more oil and fry the meatballs golden brown.

6. Transfer them onto a paper towel. In the same skillet add the red onion. Fry for 1 minute.

7. Add the tomato sauce, oregano, stock, chili, salt and pepper.

8. Cook for 2 minutes and add the meatballs. Simmer for 5 minutes.

9. In another pot, boil the ramen in salted water.

10. Drain well and add to a serving bowl.

11. Top with the meatballs with its sauce. Serve hot.

Chicken Cauliflower Curry

Chicken and cauliflower surprisingly goes well together. The texture of the cauliflower complements the chicken. Adding the peas makes it even more better.

Serving Size: 4

Cooking Time: 30 Minutes

Ingredients:

- 2 lb. chicken
- 2 cup chicken stock
- 1 cup peas
- 1 cup cauliflower florets
- 2 tsp coriander powder
- 1 tsp turmeric powder
- 2 tsp garlic powder
- Salt to taste
- 1 tsp cumin
- 2 tbsp olive oil
- 2 tsp ginger powder
- 1 cinnamon stick
- 1 cardamom
- 2 red chilies
- 3 red onion, diced
- 1 tsp red chili powder
- Fresh coriander, chopped

Instructions:

1. Discard the skin of the chicken. Discard the intestines. Cut the chicken into medium pieces.

2. In a pressure cooker add the oil and fry the red onion for 1 minute.

3. Add the ginger powder, red chili powder, cinnamon stick, cardamom, red chili powder, cumin, coriander, turmeric, garlic powder and salt.

4. Add ½ cup chicken stock and cover with lid.

5. Cook for 2 minutes. Add the chicken and stir well.

6. Cover and cook for 10 minutes.

7. Add the cauliflower, peas, the remaining stock and chilies.

8. Add the lid again and cook for another 5 minutes.

9. Add the coriander on top before serving.

Beef with Broccoli Stew

When you are making beef stew, try adding some vegetables into it. See how beautiful it turns out. I have used Broccoli, and carrots here. You can use any veggie of your choice.

Serving Size: 2

Cooking Time: 30 Minutes

Ingredients:

- 1 lb. boneless beef
- 1 cup broccoli florets, diced
- 1 cup diced onion
- 1 cup carrot, cut into circles
- 3 cup beef stock
- 1 tsp ginger paste
- 2 tbsp olive oil
- 1 tbsp chopped garlic
- 1 tsp turmeric
- 1 cinnamon stick
- Salt to taste
- 1 bay leaf
- 1 tsp paprika
- 1 tsp cumin

Instructions:

1. Cut the beef into thin strips.

2. In a pressure cooker add the beef, with bay leaf, cinnamon stick, turmeric, cumin, paprika, garlic, ginger and salt.

3. Cover and cook for 5 minutes on medium heat.

4. Add the rest of the ingredients. Stir well and add the lid again.

5. Cook for another 15 minutes on medium high heat. Serve hot.

Black Bean Soup

Do you want to have a wholesome soup that does not need any meat but tastes better than meat? Then try making black bean soup. The smoky red chili flavor makes it irresistible.

Serving Size: 6

Cooking Time: 1 hour

Ingredients:

- 6 cup black beans
- 6 cup mushroom stock
- 2tsp cumin
- 1 tsp smoked red chili powder
- 1 bell pepper, chopped
- 1 tsp cider vinegar
- 1 tbsp olive oil
- 1onion, chopped
- 3 garlic cloves, minced
- ¼ tsp chili powder
- 2 tbsp diced lemongrass
- 2 bay leaves
- 1 tablespoon dried oregano
- Salt and pepper to taste

Instructions:

1. Soak the black beans in water overnight. Drain well.

2. In a pressure cooker add all the ingredients.

3. Cover with lid and cook on low heat for 1 hour.

4. Use a hand blender to make a smooth mix.

5. Serve hot with smoked red chili powder on top.

Pan Fried Lemon Fish with Asparagus

Pan fried fish tastes good in its self anyway, but when you add lemon flavor to it, it elevates the fish. I have used butter fried asparagus on the side to give the dish some texture.

Serving Size: 3

Cooking Time: 10 Minutes

Ingredients:

- 6 white fish fillets
- 1 lemon, cut into thin slices
- ½ tsp lemon juice
- 1 tsp black pepper
- Salt to taste
- 2 tbsp butter
- Herbs of your choice, chopped

Instructions:

1. Marinate the fish fillets with the pepper, salt, and lemon juice. Let it sit for 10 minutes.

2. In a skillet melt half the butter.

3. Add the fish fillets and fry them golden brown.

4. Add the lemon slices around the fish fillets while frying. It will release an aroma.

5. Transfer the fish on to a plate.

6. Into the same skillet add the rest of the butter.

7. Add the asparagus and toss for 3-4 minutes. Sprinkle the salt and pepper on top.

8. Serve the fish with asparagus.

Classic Chicken and Egg Salad

A classic egg mayo salad can elevate by adding some chicken. You can add leftover chicken here too. The tahini flavor adds more dimension to this salad.

Serving Size: 4

Cooking Time: 20 Minutes

Ingredients:

- 4 eggs
- 2 chicken breasts
- Salt and pepper to taste
- 1 cup mayo
- 1 tbsp ginger garlic paste
- 2 green chilies, chopped
- Fresh coriander, chopped
- 1 tbsp olive oil
- 1 tsp tahini paste
- 1 tsp mustard

Instructions:

1. In a pan add the chicken with 2 tbsp chicken stock.

2. Add ginger garlic paste, some salt and pepper.

3. Cover and cook until the chicken is fully tender.

4. Transfer to a plate and shred it finely using a fork.

5. Add to a mixing bowl and set aside for now.

6. Hard boil the eggs in salted water.

7. Once they are done, drain well and pour into a cold bath.

8. Get rid of the shells. Mash them finely. Reserve one egg to garnish the salad later.

9. Add the mashed eggs into the chicken.

10. Add the coriander, chilies, mayo, tahini and mustard. Add the olive oil.

11. Mix well and serve.

Tomato Cucumber Cheese Salad

If you want to eat something to detoxify your system then this is the salad you should go for. It is super quick to make and it has many good nutrition value.

Serving Size: 1

Ingredients:

- 1 red onion, sliced
- 1 red bell pepper, sliced
- Fresh coriander, chopped
- 6-8 baby spinach
- 1/3 cup feta cheese, cut into cubes
- 1 tomato, diced
- Salt and pepper to taste
- 1 cucumber, sliced
- 1 tsp honey
- 1 tsp olive oil
- 6-8 green olives

Instructions:

1. Add all the vegetables in a mixing bowl.

2. Add the salt, pepper, feta cheese and coriander.

3. Add the olive oil and honey and toss gently. Serve.

Creamy Pumpkin Soup

Pumpkin is very good for our health and skin. I try to add pumpkin most of my dishes. This is a creamy pumpkin soup with a little bit of cinnamon and ginger flavor.

Serving size: 2-3

Cooking Time: 20 Minutes

Ingredients:

- 1 cup pumpkin puree
- A pinch of salt
- 1/2 tsp ground cinnamon
- 1 cup goat milk
- 1/2 tsp pure vanilla
- ½ cup heavy cream
- 1/4tsp ground ginger
- White pepper to taste

Instructions:

1. Add everything in a pot except the heavy cream.

2. Cover and cook for 15 minutes on medium heat.

3. Add the heavy cream and then simmer for another 5 minutes on low heat.

4. Serve hot.

Snack

Stuffed Dates with Cottage Cheese and Almonds

Muslims enjoy their dates and this appetizer is really tasty. It is the perfect party food. It is good for a game night as well. I have added pecans, but you can add almonds, cashews or even any other nuts.

Serving Size: 2-3

Ingredients:

- 8-10 Dates
- 10 toasted pecans
- A pinch of sage
- A pinch of sea salt
- 1 cup cottage cheese
- A pinch of cinnamon
- A pinch of white pepper

Instructions:

1. Cut the dates in half and then discard the pits. Make sure not to cut all the way.

2. In a bowl combine the cream cheese with sage, cinnamon, salt and pepper.

3. Mix well and stuff the dates generously.

4. Add toasted pecans on top and serve.

Homemade Hot dogs

When you want restaurant quality fast food at home, this is the recipe you should follow. Muslims enjoy their meat but because halal meat is not available everywhere all the time, they make this type of street food at home often.

Serving Size: 4

Cooking Time: 20 minutes

Ingredients:

- 1 lb. sausage
- ½ cup almond flour
- 1 egg
- ½ tsp salt
- 1½ cups shredded cheese
- 1 tsp baking powder
- 4 tbsp coconut flour
- 1 tbsp butter

Instructions:

1. Preheat the oven to 350 degrees F.

2. In a mixing bowl combine the flour with baking powder.

3. In a pan add the butter and melt over low heat. Add in the cheese and make a smooth mix.

4. Take off the heat. Add in the eggs.

5. Mix well and add the flour mix. Knead dough and roll it out thinly on a flat surface.

6. Cut into 8 squares and add sausage piece in the middle of each square and wrap tightly. Seal the edges with water carefully.

7. Do the same with the rest and add to your baking sheet.

8. Bake in the oven for 20 minutes. Serve in room temperature.

Salami and cheese chips

When you want to give yourself and your taste buds a little treat, this type of snacks you go for. It is very high in protein and enriched with flavors.

Serving Size: 2

Cooking Time: 5 minutes

Ingredients:

- ½ cup salami, about 20 slices
- 2 tbsp grated parmesan cheese
- 1 tsp paprika powder
- Salt to taste

Instructions:

1. Preheat the oven to 450 degrees F.

2. Grease your baking sheet and add parchment paper.

3. Arrange the salami onto the baking sheet.

4. Add grated cheese on top of the slices.

5. Add paprika and salt.

6. Bake in the oven for 5 minutes.

7. Serve warm.

Baked cheese

When you want your baked cheese to be healthy, you add bell pepper in it. It tastes quite good. It is good for a game night, or a party food too.

Serving Size: 1

Cooking Time: 20 minutes

Ingredients:

- 4 tbsp feta cheese
- 1 pinch chili flakes
- 2 tbsp olive oil
- Salt to taste
- 1 red bell pepper, sliced

Instructions:

1. Preheat the oven to 400 degrees F.

2. Add parchment paper on your baking dish.

3. Arrange red pepper slices and top with cheese.

4. Add the salt, chili flakes and drizzle the oil on top.

5. Bake for 20 minutes only.

6. Serve warm.

Seed crackers

Seeds are very good for our skin and health. It is enriched with flavors too. Try this next time when you crave for a snack.

Serving Size: 2

Cooking Time: 45 minutes

Ingredients:

- 1/3 cup pumpkin seeds
- 1 tsp stevia
- 1 tsp salt
- 1/3 cup almond flour
- 1/3 cup sesame seeds
- 1/3 cup sunflower seeds
- 2 tbsp coconut oil
- 1 cup boiling water
- 1/3 cup chia seeds

Instructions:

1. Preheat the oven to 300 degrees F.

2. In a bowl mix the sesame seeds, sunflower seeds, salt, pumpkin seeds, flour and chia seeds.

3. Add the boiling water, stevia and coconut oil.

4. Use a fork to mix everything together.

5. Spread them onto your baking sheet.

6. Bake in the oven for about 45 minutes.

7. Let it cool down a bit and cut into squares.

8. Serve in room temperature.

Dessert

Coconut Balls

This can be both served as a snack or as a dessert. If you have a habit of munching on something sweet, then you will love this treat. It is thousand times better than your average store bought chocolates or delights.

Serving Size: 2

Cooking Time: 20 minutes

Ingredients:

- 2 tbsp unsalted butter
- ½ tsp vanilla extract
- ½ cup shredded coconut
- ¼ tsp ground cinnamon
- ¼ tsp ground cardamom

Instructions:

1. In a skillet, add the butter.

2. Add the shredded coconut and cook until they become brown.

3. Add in the cinnamon, cardamom and vanilla.

4. Toss for 2 minutes and take off the heat.

5. Use your hands to create little balls.

6. Serve in room temperature.

Mango Coconut Ice Cream

Do you love ice cream? Try this date and mango ice cream. You would love it.

Serving Size: 2 cup

Ingredients:

- 1 tablespoon orange juice
- 1/3 cup shredded coconut
- 2 cup goat milk
- 1/2 tsp coconut extract
- 1/2 cup honey
- 1/2 cup almond milk
- 1 ½ cup mango, diced

Instructions:

1. Add the goat milk, mango, almond milk, and honey in a food processor.

2. Blend for a minute and add the coconut, orange juice and coconut extract.

3. Blend for another 10 seconds and add to your ice cream tray.

4. Let it freeze for about 6-8 hours.

Date Almond Rice Pudding

Muslims love dates. Rice pudding is one of the most eaten desserts for the Muslims. Adding fresh fruits and chopped nuts on top adds more texture to the dessert.

Serving Size: 2

Cooking Time: 30 Minutes

Ingredients:

- 1 cup brown rice
- 4-6 dates, chopped
- 1 tbsp butter
- 1/4 tsp almond extract
- 2 tbsp date paste
- 1/4 cup toasted almonds
- 3 cup goat milk
- Pinch of cinnamon powder
- Blueberries to serve

Instructions:

1. Soak the rice in water for 30 minutes.

2. Drain well and add to a pot.

3. Add the milk, butter, cinnamon, and almond extract.

4. Cook for 15 minutes on low heat.

5. Add the date paste and chopped dates.

6. Cook for another 10 minutes and add the toasted almonds.

7. Cook for 2 more minutes and take off the heat.

8. Let it cool down completely. Add blueberries on top before serving.

Cranberry Apple Dessert Risotto

Have you ever tried sweet risotto? Try this with apples and cranberries. It will blow your mind.

Serving Size: 2

Cooking Time: 30 Minutes

Ingredients:

- 3 ½ cup goat milk
- ½ cup rice
- 1 cinnamon stick
- 2 tbsp brown sugar
- 1 tbsp butter
- 1 apple, peeled
- 1 ½ cup apple cider vinegar
- ½ cup dried cranberries
- 1 pinch of salt
- Grated coconut to serve

Instructions:

1. Cut the apple into cubes.

2. Soak your cranberries for 30 minutes in boiling water.

3. Drain well and set aside for now.

4. In a pan add the butter and toss the apple cubes for 3 minutes.

5. Add the cranberries, rice and toss for another minute.

6. Add the vinegar, milk, brown sugar, cinnamon stick and mix well.

7. Keep stirring for 20 minutes on low heat.

8. When the rice is cooked completely, take off the heat.

9. Serve with more cranberries and grated coconut on top.

Split Bengal gram Bars

Muslims enjoy their homemade sweets like this one made from Bengal gram. You would not know how good it tastes until you try it yourself in the kitchen.

Serving Size: 4

Cooking Time: 30 Minutes

Ingredients:

- 2 cup split Bengal gram
- 4 tbsp clarified butter or ghee
- ½ cup pistachio, chopped
- A pinch of salt
- 1 cup sugar
- 1 tsp cinnamon
- 1 tsp cardamom

Instructions:

1. Soak the grams in water for 2 hours.

2. Drain well and add to a pressure cooker.

3. Pour enough water to cover the grams.

4. Cook for 20 minutes on high heat.

5. Use a hand blender to mash it finely.

6. In a pan, add the ghee.

7. Add the mashed gram, cardamom, cinnamon, and stir continuously for 10 minutes.

8. Add the pistachios and toss for another 3 minutes.

9. Take off the heat and let it cool down slightly.

10. Roll them out flat and cut into your desired shape.

11. Serve cold.

Pineapple Coconut Pudding

Have you paired coconut and pineapple together before? If you haven't, you are missing out on something extraordinary. Try this recipe today and see how wonderful it tastes.

Serving Size: 4

Cooking Time: 30 minutes

Ingredients:

- 2 cup low carb coconut milk
- ½ coconut flesh, thinly sliced
- 1/3 cup sliced pineapples
- ½ cup almonds, diced
- 1 tbsp coconut flour
- A pinch of kosher salt

Instructions:

1. In a pot, pour in the coconut milk.

2. Add the coconut flour, kosher salt, and coconut flesh.

3. Cook until the milk reduced in half.

4. Add the almonds and pineapples.

5. Cook for another 8 minutes.

6. Serve cold with more nuts and pineapple slices on top.

Carrot Cookie

This carrot cookie is a crunchier version of the traditional carrot cake. It takes very little hassle in the kitchen to make it and tastes great.

Serving Size: 12 cookies

Cooking Time: 15 minutes

Ingredients:

- ¾ cup almond flour
- 1 egg
- ¾ cup erythritol
- 1 tsp maple extract
- 4 tbsp butter
- ¼ cup coconut flour
- ¼ cup shredded carrot
- 1/3 cup walnuts, chopped
- ¼ tsp baking soda
- A pinch of salt

Instructions:

1. Place a silicon mat onto your baking tray.

2. Combine the fry Ingredients: in a large mixing bowl.

3. Add the egg and coat with hands.

4. Add the butter, maple extract and the rest of the Ingredients:.

5. Knead well and create sticky dough.

6. Wrap with plastic wrapper and keep in the refrigerator for 30 minutes.

7. Roll out flat and cut into rounds.

8. Add to your baking tray.

9. Bake for 15 minutes with 350 degrees F.

Conclusion

When you switch to a healthy eating habit, you will notice positive changes in your everyday activity. You will feel more energetic all through the day. You will feel less lethargic even after a hardworking day. The food you in take has a lot to do with our productivity. Try the paleo diet for 1 month straight and see how miraculously your life changes not only in terms of your body but also your mind would be fresher.

Try making the recipes by following all the steps carefully and before you will know it, your cooking will be admired by others.

Author's Afterthoughts

Thanks ever so much to each of my cherished readers for investing the time to read this book!

I know you could have picked from many other books, but you chose this one. So, a big thanks for downloading this book and reading all the way to the end.

If you enjoyed this book or received value from it, I'd like to ask you for a favor. Please take a few minutes to post an honest and heartfelt review on Amazon.com. Your support does make a difference and helps to benefit other people.

Thanks for your Reviews!

Rachael Rayner

About the Author

Rachael Rayner

Are you tired of cooking the same types of dishes over and over again? As a mother of not one, but two sets of twins, preparing meals became very challenging, very early on. Not only was it difficult to get enough time in the kitchen to prepare anything other than fried eggs, but I was constantly trying to please 4 little hungry mouths under 5 years old. Of course I would not trade my angels for anything in the world, but I had just about given up on cooking, when I had a genius idea one afternoon while I was napping beside one of my sons. I am so happy and proud to tell you that since then, my kitchen has become my sanctuary and my children have become my helpers. I have transformed my meal preparation, my grocery shopping habits, and my cooking style. I am Racheal Rayner, and I am proud to tell you that I am no longer the boring mom sous-chef people avoid. I am the house in our neighborhood where every kid (and parent) wants to come for dinner.

I was raised Jewish in a very traditional household, and I was not allowed in the kitchen that much. My mother cooked the same recipes day in day out, and salt and pepper were probably the extent of the seasonings we were able to detect in the dishes she made. We did not even know any better until we moved out of the house. My husband, Frank is a foodie. I thought I was too, until I met him. I mean I love food, but who doesn't right? He revolutionized my knowledge about cooking. He used to take over in the kitchen, because after all, we were a modern couple and both of us worked full time jobs. He prepared chilies, soups, chicken casseroles—one more delicious than the last. When I got pregnant with my first set of twins and had to stay home on bed rest, I took over the kitchen and it was a disaster. I tried so hard to find the right ingredients and recipes to make the dishes taste something close to my husband's. However, I hated follow recipes. You don't tell a pregnant woman that her food tastes bad, so Frank and I reluctantly ate the dishes I prepared on week days. Fortunately, he was the weekend chef.

After the birth of my first set of twins, I was too busy to even attempt to cook. Sure, I prepared thousands of bottles of milk and purees, but Frank and I ended up eating take out 4 days out of 5. Then, no break for this mom, I gave birth to my second set of twins only 19 months later! I knew that now it was not just about Frank and I anymore, but it was about these little ones for whom I wanted to cook healthy meals, and I had to learn how to cook.

One afternoon in March, when I got up from that power nap with my boys, I had figured out what I needed to do to improve my cooking skills and stop torturing my family with my bland dishes. I had to let go of everything I had learned, tasted, or seen from my childhood and start over. I spent a week organizing my kitchen, and I equipped myself a new blender. I also got some fun shaped cookie cutters, a rolling pin, wooden spatulas, mixing bowls, fruit cutters, and plenty of plastic storage containers. I was ready.

My oldest twins, Isabella and Sophia are now teenagers, and love to cook with their Mom when they are not too busy talking on the phone. My youngest twins Erick and John, are now 10 years old and so helpful in the kitchen, especially when it's time to make cookies.

Let me start sharing my tips, recipes, and shopping suggestions with you ladies and gentlemen. I did not reinvent the wheel here but I did make my kitchen my own, started storing my favorite baking ingredients, and visiting the fresh produce market more often. I have mastered the principles of slow cooking and chopping veggies ahead of time. I have even embraced the involvement of my little ones in the kitchen with me.

I never want to hear you say that you are too busy to cook some delicious and healthy dishes, because BUSY, is my middle name.

If you are a Muslim and living in a non-Muslim country, then getting Halal dishes is not a common scenario. You may find one or two restaurants in your city that would serve you halal food. So, to enjoy restaurant quality halal food, you need to get cooking in the kitchen!

Here you will find 30 delicious Halal recipes that range from simple to somewhat complex. Try the simple recipes first and as you grow as a cook, try the advance recipes. The book would cover your halal breakfast, lunches, dinners, snacks and even desserts.

So even if you do not have any halal restaurants near you, you can still enjoy gourmet halal food. Spend a little time in the kitchen. It will save you a lot of money. Every food store has a halal section. Make sure to shop from there to avoid any unwanted things like pork fat, alcohol, blood in your food.

ISBN 9781708318352

90000

9 781708 318352

Halal
2019

Reclaiming the Feminist Vision

Consciousness-Raising and Small Group Practice

Janet L. Freedman